The World of Mythology:
African Mythology

By Jim Ollhoff

Visit us at
WWW.ABDOPUBLISHING.COM

Published by ABDO Publishing Company, 8000 West 78th Street, Suite 310, Edina, MN 55439. Copyright ©2011 by Abdo Consulting Group, Inc. International copyrights reserved in all countries. No part of this book may be reproduced in any form without written permission from the publisher. ABDO & Daughters™ is a trademark and logo of ABDO Publishing Company.

Printed in the United States of America, North Mankato, Minnesota.
112010
122011

Editor: John Hamilton
Graphic Design: Sue Hamilton
Cover Design: Neil Klinepier
Cover Photo: Gonzalo Ordóñez
Interior Photos and Illustrations: Alamy-pgs 14, 22, 23, 27 & 28; AP-pgs 12 & 17; Corbis-pgs 11, 13, 20, 25 & 29; Getty Images-pgs 15 & 16; Granger Collection-pgs 9, 19 & 21; iStockphoto-pgs 4, 7, 10, 18 & 26; Thinkstock-pgs 5, 6, 8, 24, 30 & top/bottom border image.

Library of Congress Cataloging-in-Publication Data

Ollhoff, Jim, 1959-
  African mythology / Jim Ollhoff.
     p. cm. -- (The world of mythology)
  ISBN 978-1-61714-716-6
  1. Mythology, African--Juvenile literature. I. Title.
  BL2400.O57 2011
  398.2096--dc22
                        2010032577

CONTENTS

THE MIGHTY MYTH

There's an old African saying that goes, "God made humans, because God likes to hear stories." Humans are good at telling stories. Stories are sometimes called myths, legends, sagas, fables, or folktales. What's the difference? Actually, each of those words has a slightly different meaning. It's difficult for people to come up with exact definitions.

A myth is a story that is important to people. It might deal with gods and goddesses, or how the Earth and stars came to be. It might focus on important traits that people should have, or it might focus on a heroic journey. A good story is not always the same as a myth. A myth helps define who we are. It tells us something about what we believe, how we should act, or what kind of people we are.

Legends usually do not focus on gods and goddesses, although they can be part of the story. Sometimes, legends deal with a place, such as the legend of Atlantis. Legends are often about people. Many times, legends start with a small kernel of truth, and then get exaggerated over the years, like the legends of King Arthur or Robin Hood.

Right: Legends are often about people. They may start with truth, but then become exaggerated.

Above: A myth tells us something about what we believe, how we should act, or what kind of people we are.

Saga is a Norse word that means, "What is said." Usually, sagas are long, extended stories, often in poem form. They often deal with one person who is a central figure, like the Greek poem *The Odyssey*. That poem tells about the great quest of one man, Ulysses.

A fable is a story that is obviously fictitious. Fables often involve talking animals. They usually have a moral, an important point the storyteller wants to communicate. An example of a fable is *The Lion and the Rat*, from a collection called Aesop's Fables.

Above: The folktale of "Hansel and Gretel."

Folktales are stories that come from a particular part of the world. "Hansel and Gretel" is a folktale from Germany. Folktales usually are meant to entertain people, but they can also present an important moral.

A fairy tale is a kind of folktale. Fairy tales usually involve supernatural beings who help someone, usually a person who is poor and downtrodden. The story of "Cinderella" is a good example. These stories gave poor people hope that they might hit a stroke of luck and live happily ever after.

The definitions of these words are not set in stone. Different people use these terms in various ways. However, they do show the great diversity of stories, and how important stories are to the human spirit.

Above: In Aesop's fable "The Lion and the Rat," the lion doesn't eat the rat. Later, when the lion is captured, the rat saves the king of beasts by gnawing through a rope and freeing him.

IT ALL STARTED IN AFRICA

The first humans evolved in Africa probably between 100,000 and 200,000 years ago. As the climate changed and deserts grew, groups of humans left Africa to populate the rest of the planet. The first wave of people probably left about 60,000 years ago, going eastward toward Asia.

People started farming at least by 4000 BC, probably much earlier. The civilization called Egypt sprang up along the Nile River about 3100 BC. Tribes, villages, and kingdoms emerged all over Africa. European civilizations, such as the Greeks, Phoenicians, and Romans, tried to settle on the north coast of Africa.

Slave traders raid an African village.

Over the centuries, various African kingdoms rose and fell. The vast majority of people in Africa lived in small villages, where they farmed the land and traded with nearby villages. In the 1500s, European nations began to exploit Africa, taking out gold, ivory, and other treasures. Worst of all, slave trading became more common.

Late in the twentieth century, many African countries declared independence from European control and influence. Today, there are more than 50 African countries that continue to work toward growing economies and stable governments.

Above: Civilizations arose along the Nile River from Ethiopia to the Mediterranean Sea.

THE SOUL OF AFRICA

In many parts of the world, myths were shared from village to village, until national myths emerged. However, that happened less in Africa. Most African tribes, villages, and kingdoms had their own myths. The large deserts, mountains, and jungles of Africa kept myths and stories from being shared across the land.

Many African myths did share a few common things. There was a blending of the natural and supernatural. Africans saw the supernatural in almost everything, from gods in the trees and mountains, to spirits of ancestors living nearby. Many tribes also had myths about early wanderings. This might be because of the frequent migrations tribes made to stay close to food sources.

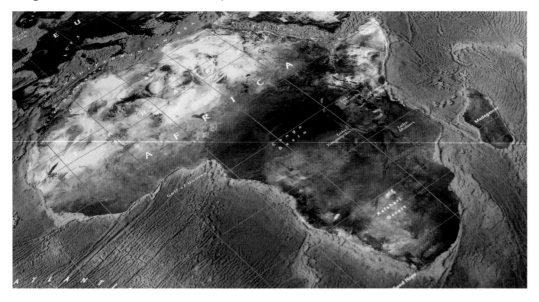

Above: Africa's large deserts, mountains, and jungles hindered myths from being shared.

Above: A dancer in an African mask. Masks may represent gods, spirits of ancestors, mythological creatures, dead animal spirits, and other powerful beings.

Mythology helped hold communities together. In many places of the world, such as Egypt or Rome, the center of the community was the temple, where stories were often shared. Throughout most of Africa, there were fewer temples, but they still had stories. In West Africa, musicians and storytellers called *griots* performed the stories and taught people the mythology. As their audience sat around the fire, the griots danced and drummed and sang stories. The people learned the myths and stories by word of mouth. Then, they passed them on to the next generation just as they had been told in generations past. Each generation had its own griots, who told the myths and stories over and over. In many places in Africa, griots were more important than priests.

Many African myths explained how the crops grew. Starvation was a constant threat, so rain-making rituals made people think they had some control over nature. Other myths celebrated the bonds of friendship.

Some myths explained the importance of cooperation within the community. It was common for African people working in the fields to sing songs as they worked. This was not just to pass the time. It was a way to bring unity to the villages and tribes.

A modern-day griot from Senegal, West Africa.

People started writing down African myths in the late 1800s and early 1900s. But there is a rich tradition of oral storytelling that still holds today in Africa.

Above: An elderly Bushman woman of the Kalahari tells a story.

CREATION STORIES

Above: A statue of Gu, a blacksmith god who prepared the world for humans.

There are many creation stories in Africa. The Dogon people of Mali said that there was a star that contained the seeds for the universe. The Fon people of West Africa talked about Gu, a blacksmith god who prepared the world for humans. The San people of the Kalahari Desert said that Dxui was the god of creation, who daily changed into a new part of nature. The Akan people of Ghana said that a moon goddess named Ngame created all things and gave birth to the sun each day. Many African cultures, such as the Lungu people of Zambia, thought that the universe was hatched from a giant egg.

Above: An African statue of mother and child. According to the Akan people of Ghana, the moon goddess named Ngame created all things.

Above: One African myth talks about Aido-Hwedo, a snake who formed the world around him.

Several cultures have stories about how a giant snake created the world. One myth talks about a serpent named Aido-Hwedo, who formed the world around him. The rivers followed his body. When he moved, he caused earthquakes. Snakes were popular in creation myths. One reason is because they shed their skin, and ancient people thought this allowed snakes to live forever.

In the area of southern Sudan, there was a myth about the first human woman. Her name was Abuk. She was also the goddess of water and gardens. The creator god allowed her to plant one grain of millet per day, and this grain provided for all her needs. However, she became greedy and wanted to plant more. As she worked in her garden, she accidentally hit the creator god in the toe. The creator god became so angry that he went back to heaven. Then he cut the rope that tied heaven and Earth together. Ever since that time, people have had to work very hard to grow crops.

Above: A Sudanese myth about an angry creator god explains why people there must work very hard to grow crops.

TRICKSTER STORIES

The trickster is a common figure in mythology. The trickster is a god, a human, or an animal that plays tricks and gets into trouble. Sometimes the trickster is a little bit evil. But usually the trickster is just trying to have some fun. Sometimes myths tell about tricksters who do good things for humanity, either by accident or on purpose. Sometimes tricksters get humans into trouble. The trickster's job is to upset the applecart of normal, everyday life. African mythology is full of tricksters, most of them animals.

One famous African trickster is Eshu, from the mythology of the Yoruba people. One day, Eshu went to the creator god and told him that thieves were planning to raid the creator's garden. That night, Eshu snuck into the creator's house and stole his shoes. Eshu put on the shoes, and then he stole vegetables out of the creator's garden. In the morning, the footprints were plain to see. The creator god measured the footprints against all the people in order to find the thief, but they fit no one. Then Eshu suggested that the creator measure the footprints of his own shoes, and they fit exactly. Eshu said that the creator must

Eshu used the creator's shoes to leave footprints in the garden.

have stolen from his own garden. The creator was angry with Eshu and accused him of setting the whole thing up. Then the creator withdrew from humanity and went to live in the sky.

Above: A statue of the famous African trickster god, Eshu.

Above: An African Savanna hare in Masai Mara National Reserve in Kenya.

Another famous trickster is Hare the rabbit, popular among many cultures in Africa. In one story, Hare's wife told him to plow his field. Hare was too lazy to do it himself, so he challenged an elephant to a tug-of-war. The elephant agreed, thinking he could easily win. But Hare also challenged a hippopotamus to a tug-of-war. Hare tied the rope to each of the animals, and then a plow to the middle of the rope. As the elephant and hippo pulled back and forth, the field got plowed.

The stories of Hare came across the Atlantic Ocean during the slave trade of the 1800s. In the American stories, Hare became known as "Brother Rabbit," or "Br'er Rabbit."

Above: Br'er Rabbit and Br'er Fox were illustrated in 1895 for the folktales written by Joel Chandler Harris. In his youth, Harris learned the tales from elderly African Americans.

DEATH AND DISEASE

A rope that ties heaven and Earth together is present in several African myths. One tale, from the Nuer people of East Africa, is about a time when there was no death, and all people lived forever. Anyone who got old could climb up the rope to heaven and would instantly become young again. One day, a hyena and a bird climbed up the rope. Since it was forbidden for animals to climb the rope, the high god said that these two animals should not be allowed to leave because if they went back to Earth, they might cause trouble. Despite the order, one night the hyena and the bird crawled back down to Earth. Once at the bottom, the hyena cut the rope. From then on, humans grew old and died because there was no way to climb into heaven.

Right: A Nuer woman. The Nuer people tell a tale that at one time there was no death. Anyone who got old could climb up the rope to heaven and would instantly become young again.

Above: According to an African tale, a hyena and a bird climbed the rope to heaven. They were not supposed to leave, but the two animals crawled back down the rope. At the bottom, the hyena cut the rope. From then on, humans grew old and died because there was no way to climb into heaven.

Some African stories tried to explain why bad things happen. Many stories said that certain people were born with the "evil eye." They weren't bad people, and they didn't know they had the evil eye. But their mere presence in a room could cause expensive pots to fall off shelves or things to go missing.

Above: Some African stories told of people born with the "evil eye."

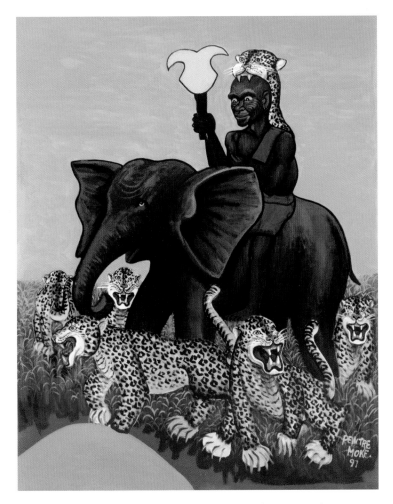

Left: Bad things were sometimes blamed on sorcerers. It was said that these magicians could make people sick or die.

Other bad things were blamed on sorcerers. These magicians could make people sick or die. The sorcerers ate the souls of the living to gain spiritual strength. Some sorcerers, it was said, dug up dead bodies and turned them into zombies.

One story, told by the Hausa people of Nigeria, is about an evil sorceress who used poison to kill people. The sorceress was planning to kill her own husband and father-in-law. She filled their soup with poison and set the bowls in front of them. However, the soup came to life and warned the men not to eat. They threw the poisoned soup at the sorceress. The poison made dozens of mouths appear all over her body. She was banished from the town and was never heard from again.

POPULAR GODS AND GODDESSES

The myths of Africa have been passed down for centuries, told and retold by many generations. In this land where human beings first arose, many of the myths tell of the creation of the world.

Chuku: The supreme creator of the Ibo people of North Africa was Chuku, also called the Great Spirit. When people first started to die in the world, Chuku told a sheep to run to Earth and give people a message. When somebody dies, Chuku said, the people should put the body on the ground and then cover it with ashes. The person would then come back to life. But the sheep mixed up the story. Instead, he told people to burn the bodies to ashes and bury them in the Earth. Since that time, people have been mortal.

Right: A sheep was told by Chuku, the Great Spirit of the Ibo people, to give the people a message. But the sheep mixed it up, causing people to be mortal.

Cagn: The creator god of the San people of the Kalahari Desert was Cagn. He could take the form of any animal. He spent time as a praying mantis, an antelope, and a caterpillar. He could even turn his shoes into wild dogs that protected him.

Above: Cagn, the creator god, was said to be able to take the form of any animal.

Mboom: The Kuba people of central Africa told the story of the creator god Mboom, who had nine children. He gave each of these nine children the name "Woot." Each child created a different part of the world. Death came into the world when Woot, the god of sharp blades, killed his brother Woot, the god of thorns, after a fierce argument.

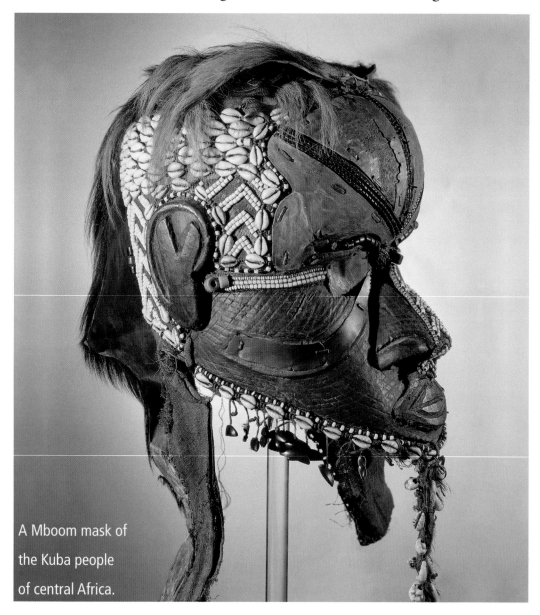

A Mboom mask of the Kuba people of central Africa.

Unkulunkulu: The Zulus of southern Africa had a god known as the "old, old one," or Unkulunkulu. He created humans out of grass. Then he told a lizard to pass a message to humans that they would be immortal. The lizard moved too slowly, so Unkulunkulu got angry and told another lizard that humans would eventually die. The second lizard got to the humans first. However, Unkulunkulu felt bad and wanted to help people, so he taught them about marriage and friendship. He told people that after death, they would live in the sky. The stars in the nighttime sky, according to the Zulus, are ancestors who look down on the world.

Above: A lizard was sent by Unkulunkulu with a message that humans would be immortal. The lizard moved too slowly. Unkulunkulu got angry and sent a second lizard with the message that humans would eventually die.

GLOSSARY

ATLANTIS

A legendary island with a mysterious lost civilization that sank to the bottom of the ocean thousands of years ago, never to be found again. Some believe Atlantis was fiction, while others believe the story to be true. People have searched for the lost island for hundreds of years.

BLACKSMITH

A person who uses fire, hammer, and an anvil to make and repair things made from iron and other metals.

CREATION

How the universe, the world, and people came into being.

GRIOTS

West African musicians and storytellers who perform and teach people the mythology and stories of their culture.

IMMORTAL

Being able to live forever. Many African myths begin their creation story with humans being immortal.

KING ARTHUR

The legendary warrior-king of the Britons who lived in the city of Camelot and ruled with his Knights of the Round Table.

ROBIN HOOD

A legendary English hero and outlaw. He was known for taking from the rich and giving to the poor.

SORCERER

Someone who can perform magic for evil purposes.

TRICKSTER

A god, a human, or an animal that plays tricks and gets into trouble. The trickster is sometimes evil, but usually is just trying to have some fun.

ZOMBIES

A zombie is a person who is neither dead nor alive; the undead. In folklore, zombies are walking corpses. They have died, but have been awakened through supernatural means.

INDEX